My Cat's Not Fat, He's Just Big Boned

FALL to YOUR KNEES.

CAT ADORATION DAY.

OTHER BOOKS BY
NICOLE HOLLANDER

I'm in Training to Be Tall and Blonde

Ma, Can I Be A Feminist and Still Like Men?

That Woman Must Be on Drugs

Mercy, It's the Revolution and I'm in My Bathrobe

My Weight Is Always Perfect for My Height—Which Varies

Hi, This Is Sylvia

Sylvia on Sundays

Okay, Thinner Thighs for Everyone

Never Take Your Cat to a Salad Bar

The Whole Enchilada

Tales From the Planet Sylvia

You Can't Take it With You, So Eat it Now

Everything Here is Mine

Female Problems: An Unhelpful Guide

My Cat's Not Fat, He's Just Big-Boned

by Nicole Hollander

SOURCEBOOKS HYSTERIA™
AN IMPRINT OF SOURCEBOOKS, INC.®
NAPERVILLE, ILLINOIS

Published by Hysteria, an imprint of Sourcebooks, Inc.
P.O. Box 4410, Naperville, Illinois 60567-4410
(630) 961-3900
Fax: (630) 961-2168
www.sourcebooks.com

ISBN-13: 978-1-4022-0861-4
ISBN-10: 1–4022-0861-8

Printed and bound in the United States of America
CH 10 9 8 7 6 5 4 3 2 1

this book is dedicated to
Eric, IZZY And Buddy...
As BiG as they wanna Be.

A WOMAN PLEADS WITH HER CAT TO HELP CURB HER WANTON SPENDING.

I CAN'T BELIEVE IT. EVERY MONTH I USE MY CREDIT CARD LIKE A MANIAC. I CAN NEVER PAY OFF THE BALANCE, SO I END UP WITH HUGE INTEREST PAYMENTS. CAN YOU GIVE ME A POST-HYPNOTIC SUGGESTION TO END THIS MADNESS?

YOU WILL SLEEP NOW, AND WHEN YOU AWAKEN, YOU WILL FEED ME FRIED CHICKEN WHEN I BLINK ONCE, AND TUNA WHEN I BLINK TWICE.

Hi, SWEET BOYS. WHAT'S UP?

CATS TEND TO MISBEHAVE WHEN FACED WITH DIVORCE, MOVING,

RENOVATION,

DON'T WORRY. I'M NOT GOING ANYWHERE.

OR IF THEIR OWNER GOES ON A LONG

TRIP.

REALLY, THERE'S NO NEED TO WORRY.

THANK YOU...

BUT WE'VE ALREADY MISBEHAVED.

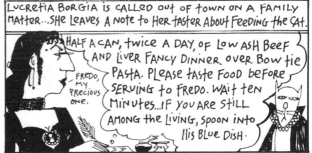

AN ALERT CAT SAVES HIS MISTRESS FROM THE MACHINATIONS OF A SINISTER SPOUSE.

OUT OF THE CORNER OF MY EYE, I SAW HER HUSBAND SLIP A VIAL OF UNTRACEABLE POISON INTO THE SUGAR-FREE SAUCE HE WAS POURING OVER A PLATE OF WHOLE-WHEAT, FAT-FREE PANCAKES. AS HE SET THE PLATE IN FRONT OF HER I SLID ACROSS THE TABLE, KNOCKING THE DISH ONTO HER LAP, SAVING HER FROM A GRUESOME DINING EXPERIENCE AND CERTAIN DEATH. SHE SHOT ME A LOOK OF GRATITUDE AS SHE LEFT THE ROOM TO SOAK HER SILK SLACKS.

We Dream each other's Dreams.

I'M LOW ON GAS.

I USED TO DREAM OF SMALL FURRY CREATURES STRUGGLING VAINLY TO ELUDE MY IMPLACABLE EMBRACE. NOW I HAVE VISIONS OF MERGERS IN WHICH I AM REPLACED BY...

AN MBA FRESH OUT OF SCHOOL. I HATE IT.

BETSY, I DREAMT I SWALLOWED A FLY.

BIRD BATH MR. CUTE

CASTLE KITTY LITTER

14

Cat Problems

A WOMAN FROM CLEVELAND WRITES: "MY DOG LOVES TO RIDE IN THE CAR, but ANY TIME I PUT MY CAT IN THE CAR, HE LETS OUT THIS TERRIBLE HIGH-PITCHED SCREAM."

A CAT REPLIES

OF course your dog Likes to ride in the CAR. tell me something A dog won't do. Your cat is terrified. He UNDERSTANDS that His life HANGs in the bALANCe every time He rides with you.

Next time throw him the keys, Let Him drive.

CATS AND OWNERS WHO ARE REALLY close sometimes DREAM EACH OTHER'S DREAMS.

I DREAMED I CLEANED the RATHROOM tiles with A toothBRUSH AND then I... Got DOWN ON MY HANDS AND KNEES AND SCRUBBED the FLOOR. I DON'T EVEN HAVE HANDS AND KNEES.

YUCK! I JUST DREAMED I HAD the HEAD OF A Love-Bird IN MY MOUTH AND I FELT BLISSFUL.

HONEY, I'M GOING to sleep ON the COUCH.

FROM THE BOOK OF HEROIC CATS

ON EASTER I disGuised MYSELF AS A BUNNY to KEEP tABS ON MY MISTRESS'S SLIMY SWAIN. HUNDREDS OF CHILDREN WERE GAMBOLING ON THE LAWN... PART OF OUR ANNUAL EGG-ROLLING PARTY... SO I WAS ALREADY QUITE CRANKY WHEN I SPIED HER SMARMY SWEETHEART SELECTING EGGS MARKED WITH A tINY RED "P," POISON! AND PUTTING THEM IN HER EASTER BASKET. NO tIME to GRIND MY tEETH. I SPED ACROSS THE LAWN, SCATTERING CHILDREN, EGGS AND THE OCCASIONAL BIRD IN MY WAKE. I RUSHED HIM OFF HIS FEET, INTO THE PUNCH BOWL. SHE PRETENDED to BE MIFFED, BUT LATER WHISPERED: "WELL DONE, DRAGONSLAYER!"

the MALICIOUS CAT writes in his JOURNAL

3:00 A.M. SUNDAY: Got up on the top of the stove, pried up one of the burner grates, dropped it, CLANG! Did it a few more times until she woke up and ran into the kitchen wild-eyed with her hair standing on end... wished I had a camera.

RASHOMON FOR CATS

Killer Bees invaded the House... I leapt into their midst with the speed of a cheetah and the moves of Steven Seagal. She was shoveling bee bodies out of the living room for weeks.

EL FEARLESS

this Decrepit Bee wandered into the house. I think Buddy sat on him accidentally. I had to give him a Valium.

21

OUR HAPPINESS IS THEIR WHOLE LIFE.

SHE bought me this AQUARIUM VIDEO-TAPE. I'VE Got A Good HEART. I Go up to the t.v. SET, I PAW the Screen pretending I'm trying to CATCH the FISH, I MAKE FELINE HUNTING SOUNDS. IF there's A KITTY HEAVEN, I'M IN.

He's so cute, he watches that video for hours.

A CAT COMPLAINS About CRUEL CAT OWNERS.

they NAMED ME "SEX MACHINE." you know, After the James Brown Song, sort of A JOKE At My Expense, right? So when I HAVE to Go to the vet AND SHE ASKS MY NAME,

they LOSE their NERVE... they TELL her: "Frisky." It ISN'T ENOUGH I HAVE to Go to the vet, I HAVE to HAVE AN identity crisis too? I could spit.

22

Severe disappointments in the Lives of Cats

Guys, Here's the NEW Addition to our FAMILY.

WHAT the heck is it?

too big to Fit in a dish, too small to use a can opener, must be a baby.

BiLinguaL CAT Lies

they kept me up all night!

No, I did not have a Group of friends over for a Late Night snack of tuna molé, Nor did we break a catnip piñata and howL olé at the moon. Perhaps you had a nightmare.... perhaps you ate a bad taco.

señor cat

HEARTBREAKING COMPLAINTS OF CATS

Hi, Sweet Boys
what can I do
for you this
fine
morning?

We need BACK-
to-school
clothes and
a box of...

New
CRAY-
ONS.

Boys, I don't
know how to
tell you this...
you're not
kids, you're
cats.

OH.

Then
I guess
we
need...

I'm sorry.
I thought
you knew.

Back-to-school
clothes and
a box of..

Mice.

Hi, this is the Sylvia Stress Reduction
Hotline. At the sound of the beep,
repeat after me: "This week, Let
someone else strive for excellence."

Ring! Ring!

CATS WHO EDUCATE THEMSELVES

CATS with **Special Powers**

CAVIAR? I HEAR AND OBEY, MASTER.

I'D LiKE to HAVE A MORE HEALTHY LifestyLe, but WHEN I GET HOME FROM WORK I eND UP sitting iN FRONT oF the t.V. eAtiNG MACAROONS.

- YOU WiLL SLeeP NOW, AND WHeN YOU AWAKEN YOU'LL beLieve tHAt COMBiNG MY FUR HAS the SAME effeCt ON YOUR HeALTH AS 30 MiNUtes OF ExeRCise AND tHRee SeRViNGS OF FRUiT AND VEGEtABLes.

FURtHeR News FROM the CAts WHO tAUGHt themseLVes to ReAD AND WHO LiKe to ORDeR FROM CAtALOGs.

YOU KNOW tHAt MAGAZiNe, the New YORKeR? WeLL, YOU CAN ORDeR StUFF FROM them too.

AND they HAVe stoRies.

HONEY, DiD YOU ORDeR 12 AGeD FiLet MiGNON SteAKs, A BROCHURe ON ExPeDitiONs to MACHU PicCHU AND A VeRMONT SMOKeD HAM?

Dear John, PLeeze, I HATE it WHEN people BLAMe their LACK OF A SOCIAL LiFe ON their CATS. Like ALL CATS, He LiVes ONLY to MAKe You HAPPY. IN this CASe, He is PROtecting YOU FROM the KNOWLeDGe tHAT NO ONe eVeR CALLs you. He doesN't WANT you to ReALIZe the FULL extent OF YOUR UNPOPU-LARity, SO He tURNS OFF tHe MACHiNe. Be GRATeFuL, YOU CAD.

love, S'yl.

this is YOUR CAT'S BRAIN ON CATNIP.

I FIND the StUDY OF BIRDS FASCINATING. HOW REWARDING to observe their FLIGHt PATTERNS, NESTING AND FEEDING HABits, the tRAINING OF their YOUNG, the beHAVIOR OF MALES AND FEMALES... AND, OF course, they're Quite YUMMY.

A VIGILANT CAT SAVES HIS MISTRESS FROM CERTAIN DEATH, YET AGAIN.

FROM the CORNER OF MY eye, I SPY HER SVELTE SWINE OF A HUSBAND POURING WHAT He SAYS ARE AMINO ACIDS INTO HER tofu SURPRISE. I THINK NOT. I LEAP OFF the CREDENZA ONTO the LIQUOR CABINET, SENDING BOTTLES OF SINGLE-MALT WHISKEY INTO THE AIR LIKE GUIDED MISSILES.

ONE OF THEM KNOCKS HIM COLD. SHE MURMURS, "POOR BABY," AND SHOOTS ME A WINK AND A GRIN. He MUSTN'T KNOW WE KNOW.

Hi, BOYS. WHAT'S UP?

MAYBE YOU DON'T LOVE US?

YOU DON'T TALK BABY TALK TO US ANYMORE...

Don't LOVE YOU? I ADORE YOU BOTH. You're MY INNER CHILD, MY DELIGHT, MY BEST PALS!

OF OUR CHARMS.

MAYBE You've TIRED...

GOSH, THIS HAS REALLY THROWN ME FOR A LOOP.... I'VE LET YOU DOWN.

the DRAPES, AND the LALIQUE.

KEEP THAT IN MIND WHEN YOU SEE the KITCHEN...

44

CATS IN CRISIS

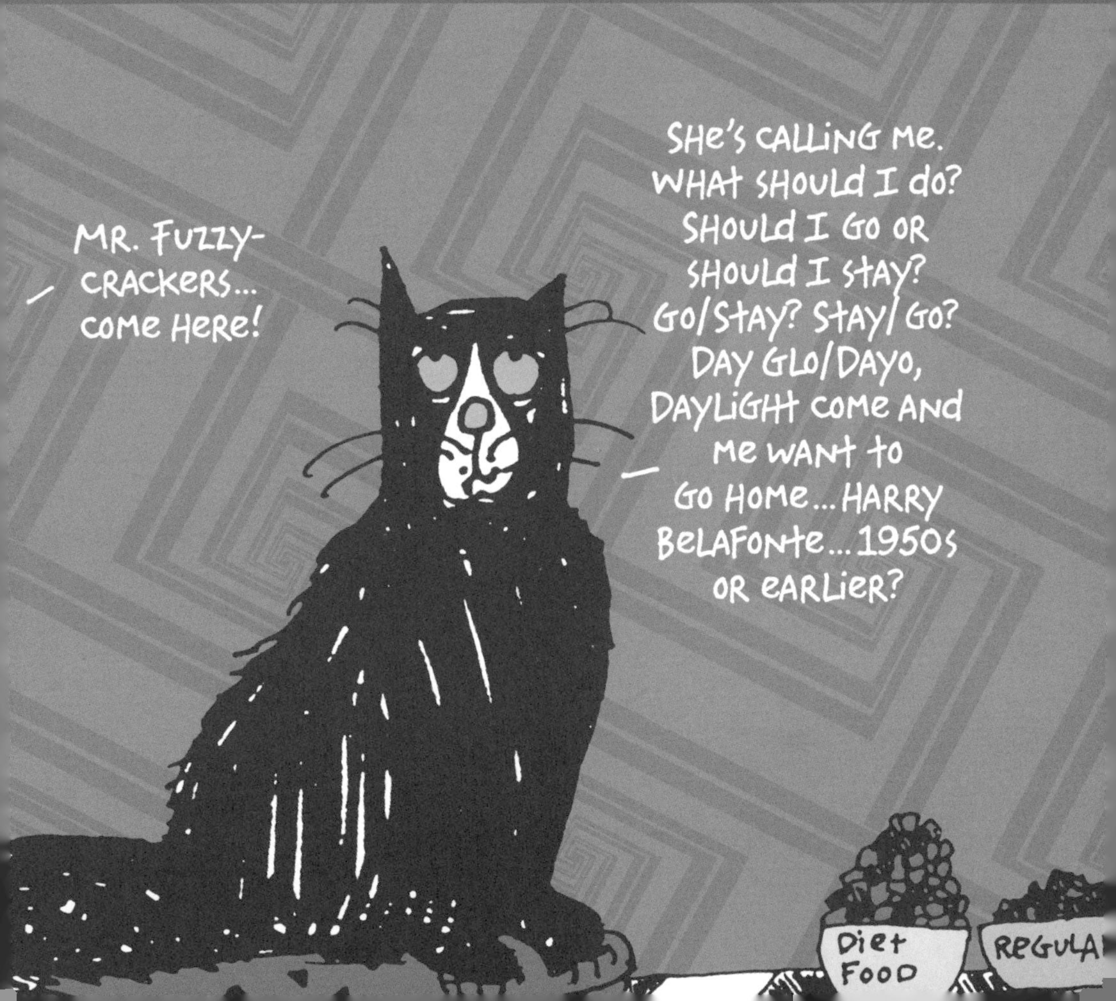

Cats who try to Manipulate their owners.

You will bring me chicken nuggets.

Forget it.

You know... when you leave in the morning, we think you're hunting. If you don't return at the usual time, we assume you've been eaten by a larger animal. Remember that when you're tempted to stop off after work for dinner and a movie.

We get anxious and our fur falls out.

Cats like to eat first thing in the morning.

I'm tired. I didn't sleep well last night.

FEED US NOW.

I'm just going to drop off for a minute.

WE HAVE YOUR HUSBAND.

RASHOMON FOR CATS

I WANT to GO OUTSIDE. I WANT to ROAM FREE, FEEL the WIND IN MY HAIR... birds IN MY teeth.

But SHE KEEPS ME A PRISONER HERE, AGAINST MY NATURE.

I LET HER OUT IN THE BACKYARD ONCE, BUT A LEAF FELL ON HER AND SHE HID UNDER the COUCH FOR A week.

TERRIBLY MEAN CAT LIES.

WHERE ARE MY LENSES?

I'M SURE I DON'T KNOW. I HAVE NO USE FOR GREEN CONTACT LENSES. MY EYES ARE NATURALLY GREEN. I'M NOT THE ONE WITH THE WASHED OUT BABY-BLUES. HAVE YOU LOOKED IN YOUR HANDBAG? YOU COULD LOSE A STATION WAGON IN there.

51

54

Cats are more resistant to having their teeth brushed than dogs, but tricks can be used.

She walks toward me. Her right hand is wrapped in a cloth that smells like it's been dipped in clam juice. I swear I had no idea that she wanted to clean my teeth. I didn't know what she was going to do. It seemed kinky to me, so I bit her.

When you need dentures, don't come whining to me.

PHIL

A cat suffers fallout from the war on drugs

So she says I can't have catnip any more because it's like a drug. So, like, what's she worried about. I'm not going to do well in school or what?

56

EDGAR, come AND meet the puppy I bought to keep you company.

the word "Betrayal" Leaps to mind, but doesn't quite conjure up the Full Horror of what has occurred here today.

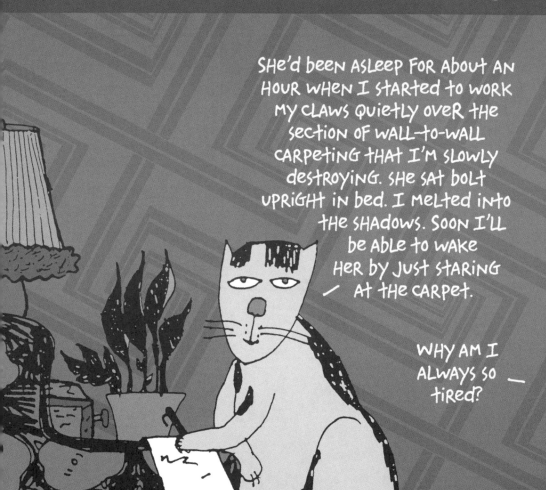

Literary Cat Lies.

the SEQUEL to "GONE with the WIND" WILL HAVE CATS reprising the MAIN roles.

CHAPTER 1. ASHLEY NARROWLY escapes NeuteriNg, ANd AtLaNta BurNs.

Hi GUYS!
DID I HEAR the PHONE RING?

FEED US. NOW.

MAYBe.

WHO WAS it? ROGER? Does He WANt me to CALL Him?

FEED US. MEMORY CELLS FADING FAST.

SOMEthiNg RATHER URGENT.

OKAY, Here's YOUR FOOD. WHO CALLED? WAS it BILL?

Got ANY MORE of those LittLe...

COCKtAIL FRANKS AROUND?

DAVE

FRED

63

64

CATS LIKE YOU TO COME HOME RIGHT AFTER WORK.

AFTER WORK WE'RE GOING TO HAVE DINNER AND SEE THAT NEW PLAY EVERYONE'S TALKING ABOUT... I HAVEN'T HAD A NIGHT OUT IN AGES. I'M SO EXCITED.

YOU WILL SLEEP NOW, AND WHEN YOU AWAKEN, YOU WILL HAVE NO MEMORY OF MY INSTRUCTIONS... BUT TONIGHT, AS THE CURTAIN RISES, YOU WILL HURRY FROM THE THEATER, STOPPING ONLY TO PURCHASE A CAN OF TUNA, WHICH YOU WILL STUFF INTO YOUR TINY EVENING BAG AND BRING TO ME.

CATS SPEAK OUT ON MUSIC.

WE FIND THE HUMAN SINGING VOICE SOMEWHAT UNPLEASANT. OF COURSE, THERE'S NOT MUCH WE CAN DO ABOUT THAT NOW.

HUMANS LISTEN TO MANY DIFFERENT KINDS OF MUSIC... THAT'S WHY THEY'RE SO STRESSED OUT.

WHEN CATS RULE THE WORLD, EVERYONE WILL LISTEN EXCLUSIVELY TO GERSHWIN... MAYBE A LITTLE COLE PORTER.

OH NO, THEY CAT TAKE THAT AWAY FROM ME.

Cats who Procrastinate

SHE LEFT A BOX OF GRANOLA ON the COUNTER this MORNING. WE'RE GOING to DRAG it INTO the LIVING ROOM, RIP it OPEN... GRANOLA ALL over the CARPET. then we're GOING to ROLL IN the STUFF, GRINDING the NUTS AND RAISINS INTO the RUG. BUT FIRST we NEED A NAP.

TIMING IS EVERY-THING.

EDGAR...

WHEN SHE CALLS ME, I LIKE to WAIT JUST LONG ENOUGH SO SHE CAN'T TELL WHETHER I CAME because SHE CALLED OR because I JUST WANDERED by ON SOME MYS-TERIOUS BUSINESS OF MY OWN.

BILLY...

HERE I AM. PANT, PANT I HOPE I DIDN'T KEEP YOU WAITING, YOUR WORSHIP. ARF, ARF.

A CAT WEIGHS HIS OPTIONS

It's 3:00 A.M. I'm awake and he's asleep— what's wrong with this picture? If I wake him, he'll never get back to sleep and he'll be very irritable at the office tomorrow, but hey, I don't have to work with him, so the question is should I turn on the dishwasher or the t.v.?

A Cat Therapist Responds

Going to the vet combines several activities that are traumatic for cats: leaving the house, riding in a moving metal deathtrap, and being touched by a stranger who smells like a dog. The humane solution is to have the vet come to the house, no matter what it costs.

My boyfriend's best friend is allergic to cats. I read that if you wash a cat once a month, it reduces the allergen produced by the cat's oil glands.

Her Cats Respond

Happy to cooperate.

Eager to please.

One stipulation...

Your boyfriend joins us in the tub.

A cat discusses the new "Lite" cat foods.

I have only two pleasures in life, standing on the newspaper while you're trying to read it, and eating.

Leave my food alone. If I need a kitty by-pass, I'll pay for it myself.

FROM the JOURNAL OF AN insincere CAT

Rita, Honey, could you turn up the thermostat?

It's as high as it goes.

I found out today that one cat, operating on his own, can decimate the bird population of a whole neighborhood. I was shocked and saddened. Those cats should be forced to wear bells, enormous bells, around their necks. I must stop writing now and brood.

LEW

L'EAU

Rewriting Robert Fulghum for the Feline Market.

Clean your fur, throw-up.

Take a nap. Take another nap.

Kitty litter then & now.

Share nothing.

HAIRBALLS Volume I

DISLOYAL CATS prevent their owners from being confirmed to top Government posts.

He smoked marijuana several times in the 60's, and was present at a party where he got a contact high in the 70's.

I never enjoyed it.

A cat is always thinking of others.

Get away from that t.v.! Move it, wouldya!

Night after night I stand here, blocking the t.v. screen, hoping those two cretins, whom I live only to love, will pick up a book.

WOKE UP AT 3:00 A.M. THIS MORNING. MANAGED TO DRAG THE RALPH LAUREN "RUSSIA" COLLECTION BED LINENS, THE CAVALRY TWILL THROW WITH FAUX PERSIAN LAMB EDGING, AND SOME OF THOSE RUFFLED PILLOWS OUT OF THE GUEST BEDROOM AND INTO THE KITTY LITTER.... SO EXHAUSTED I BARELY MANAGED TO STUFF THE CUT-VELVET DUVET INTO THE AQUARIUM BEFORE I FELL ASLEEP.

the PROBLEM AS SHE SEES it

At 3:00 A.M. He starts knocking stuff off the dresser. He stands on my chest. I'm at my wit's end. I don't get any sleep. He's driving me crazy.

the CAT'S Point of View.

I'M AWAKE At 3:00 A.M...

WHAT AM I supposed to do, read a book?

A CAT therapist Speaks:

Adapt to your cat's schedule. If you go to sleep earlier— say, right after work, you'll find yourself rarin' to go at 3:00 A.M.

the Kitty Olympics

We started slowly, kicking a small amount of litter onto the floor near the box. During the week we subtly increased the amount until...

there was as much on the floor as there was in the box. Now we're going for distance.

Bi-Lingual Cat Lies.

WOMAN FINDS PYRAMID IN ATTIC.

We didn't do it. WHATEVER YOU FIND ON THE COUCH. IT WASN'T US. WE WERE ELSE WHERE AT the time.

— oui

Cats who have their own Agendas

I've Got to take SOME CLOTHES to the CLEANERS, AND then I THOUGHT I'D GO to the LiBRARY AND PiCK UP the LATEST RoBeRt WALLER AND READ ALL AFTERNOON.

You will sleep Now, AND WHEN You AWAKEN, YOU'LL WANT to take ME to the AQUARIUM... tHere, You'LL WAit FOR ME iN the CAR WiTH the MOTOR ON. iF ANYONE TRiES to Stop us, You WiLL MOW THEM DOWN.

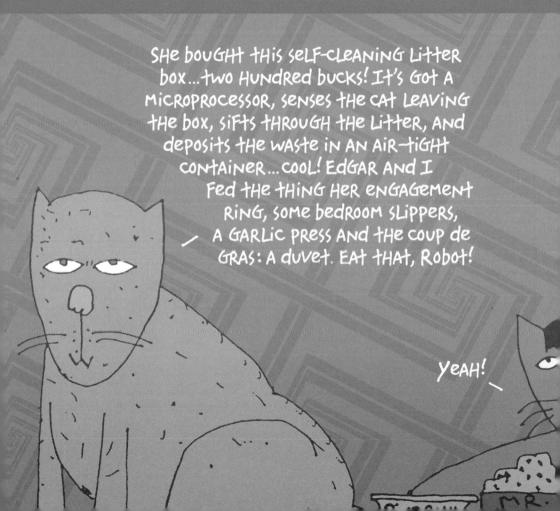

Don't ask your cat a question you already know the answer to.

—HUNGRY!

So she tells me about this springer spaniel... sweet disposition, leash-trained, "Can we bring him into our home?"

I say, "Sure bring him along—I eat springer spaniels for breakfast."

I think Cyclops would love some company.

MR. "C"

MINE

CATS who Dream their owners' Dreams.

You're having a nightmare.

NEW BRAKES? NEW SHOCKS? NO! PLEASE!

I used to dream about rooms full of hyper-active mice... plates of chicken fried golden brown...

Now I dream about shared sacrifice and I have no idea what it means. I hate that.

Honey, I just had the wierdest dream about mice. Yuck.

Good morning, boys.

Do you know what tomorrow is?

It's Father's Day.

Who told you? I didn't think you'd ever find out.

We'll never...

Be fathers.

I feel very guilty.

Try to remember that when you see the couch.

And the drapes.

From the Diary of a Vampire cat, who suffers in much the same way as Brad Pitt in "Interview with the Vampire."

I've killed many a bird. But rest assured, I get no pleasure from it. Remember, before you judge me, that I could have sunk my tiny fangs into a golden retriever or a pony...

Dooming them to an endless search for prey along the streets of New Orleans and Paris... but that would have made me even more remorseful and where's the fun in that?

Dear CAT LADY,

MY CAT HAS been in the BASEMENT FOR weeks. LAST NIGHT I STOOD At the top OF the STAIRS AND SAID, "Hey KITTY, KITTY," BUT He didN't RESPOND. I THOUGHT I HEARD MUSIC AND THEN SOMEONE SAID, "COME ON DOWN, HONEY."

EVERY EVENING I put his FOOD At the top of the STAIRS. IN the MORNING the bowl is UNTOUCHED. Now the DOG HAS DISAPPEARED. WHAT SHOULD I DO?

the Malicious cat Writes in his Journal

SHE WAS RUNNING LATE THIS MORNING. I DON'T KNOW WHY THAT BRINGS OUT MY DARK SIDE. I tried to trip Her on the stairs AND I pushed Her keys into the litter box. MAYBE I NEED kitty psychoanalysis...OR MAYBE I'M SUFFERING FROM A chicken NUGGEt DEFICIENCY.

A CAT COMPLAINS IN HIS Secret JOURNAL.

WEDNESDAY: HEARD the key in the lock... SHE WAS HOME EARLY! I'D JUST been forging Her name to a check...NO time to slip it BACK into the DRAWER..

I HAD TO PRETEND I WAS UP there trying to knock over a vase of FLOWERS. I FELT DEMEANED.

GENERAL JOSEPH ASHLY AND the FAMILY CAT took a 200-SEAT AIR FORCE PLANE FROM ITALY to COLORADO that COST MR. AND MRS. TAXPAYER $116,000!

I'M GOING to CHECK ON CHEAP FLIGHTS to COLORADO...

YOU WILL SLEEP NOW, AND WHEN YOU AWAKEN, YOU'LL ORDER A C-141 to TAKE US HOME....AND MAKE SURE there's PLENTY OF TUNA ON BOARD.

Hi, BOYS. WHAT'S ON YOUR MIND?

A HEALTH PLAN.

WE WERE WONDERING IF WE HAVE...

YES. IF YOU GET SICK, I WILL DO ABSOLUTELY EVERYTHING to MAKE YOU WELL, NO MATTER WHAT it COSTS.

EVERYTHING?

HOW MUCH IS EVERYTHING?

IF ONLY SHEEP GLAND INJECTIONS WOULD SAVE YOU, I'D FLY YOU TO A CLINIC IN LUCERNE.

FIRST CLASS?

WOULD THAT BE...

95

A CAT therapist responds

WHAT DO YOU MEAN, YOUR FIANCÉ IS ALLERGIC TO CATS? THAT'S LIKE SAYING YOUR FIANCÉ IS MARRIED OR HAS A CLOSET FULL OF WOMEN'S SHOES. WHERE WERE YOUR CATS WHEN HE CAME OVER FOR DINNER... IN TOLEDO? THE WHOLE THING SOUNDS FISHY TO ME. GIVE BACK THE RING.

the MALICIOUS CAT WRITES iN HiS JOURNAL

BEFORE the SUN WAS UP I HAD the KNOBS OFF the t.v. AND the STOVE; took HER CHARGE CARDS, HER DRIVER'S LICENSE...A PAIR OF PANTY-HOSE, the LATE NOTICES FOR the PHONE AND CABLE t.v. ... SHOVED EVERYTHING iNTO the disposal AND turNED iT ON. SHE WAS iN the KitCHEN LIKE A SHOT! WHAT A MOMENT... HER EYES WERE LIKE BILLIARD BALLS. I WISHED I HAD A CAMCORDER.

GULLible CAT owNers.

Hi.

WOULD YOU LIKE A CUP OF COFFEE?

I SURE WOULD.

REGULAR? DECAF? CON LECHÉ? ESPRESSO? TURKISH?

YOU'RE JUST PULLING MY CHAIN, RIGHT?

CORRECT.

A tiny Selection of Dog Cartoons.

THE DOGS FROM HELL TRY TO LURE GULLIBLE BURGLARS INTO THEIR CONDO.

it's too hot to go on.

think anybody's in there?

is anyone home?

NOBODY HERE BUT TWO ANCIENT COCKER SPANIELS NIBBLING AT A BOWL OF DRY FOOD FOR THE LESS-ACTIVE DOG.

COME IN QUIETLY... LOUD NOISES MAKE US TREMBLE.

THOR

DOGS WHO LIVE FOR LOVE AND THE CATS WHO MALIGN THEM.

THROW A DOG A BALL AND HE'LL FETCH IT OVER AND OVER, WEARING THAT SAME...

EXPECTANT DOPEY DOG LOOK LONG AFTER MORE ADVANCED CREATURES HAVE TIRED OF THE GAME.

LIKE HE CAN'T SPEND A WHOLE DAY STARING AT A SPOT ON THE WALL... OH, NO, I DIDN'T MEAN THAT... BAD DOG! I DON'T DESERVE HIS LOVE.

BLACKIE

RALPH

The **DOGS** FROM **HELL** Attempt to LuRE MEMBERS OF the LoYAL opposition to their CONDo.

REPUBLICANS SWEEP CONGRESS!

REPUBLICANS WIN BIG!

Pre-Election Celebration! ALL Welcome! Speeches, PAC MONEY, PRIZES, GLoATING... INDOOR GOLF!

ANYONE COMING?

FOUR GUYS WITH TINY FLAGS IN THEIR LAPELS... Get the CONDIMENTS!

the Fourth Dog

by Sylvia Lake

I PULLED the ANONY-MOUS LETTER out of the TINY DOG'S MOUTH. IT SAID: "I KNOW WHAT HAPPENED to YOUR AUNT JULIA At HoOVER DAM..."

"IF YOU WANT This to REMAIN OUR SECRET, GivE the DOG A CASHIER'S check FoR $10,000 AND A biscuit." I EXAMINED the MESSAGE cLoSELY. the lETTERS SEEMED to HAVE been cut FRoM BACK issues of the LONDON TIMES AND the NEW YORK POST. THAT RANG A bELL ....

the Dogs from HELL Attempt to Lure Pro-crastinators to their CONDO.

PLANNED to send out CHRISTMAS CARDS with CHARM-ING FAMILY PHOTO on the FRONT? HAVEN'T DONE A thing About it?? Don't WORRY! WE'LL DO IT ALL AND WRITE A PERSONAL NOTE ON EACH CARD.

ANYONE COMING?

TWO HARRIED-LOOKING WOMEN CLUTCHING FAMILY PHOTOS, HEADED this WAY...

REASON 372: WHY CATS ARE NOT COMFORTABLE At the Vets.

I DON'T KNOW WHY it is, but HE HATES CATS. HE JUST WANTS TO KILL THEM WHEN He sees them.

WHAT is the TENSILE STRENGTH OF THIS CARRIER?

the Woman who does Everything More Beautifully than you has more adorable pets than you do.

SUZI
LORD JEFF
yeats

TUESDAY: RICHARD AVEDON CALLED THIS MORNING. He's terribly eager to PHOTOGRAPH Suzi, LORD JEFF AND yeats FOR A book He's DOING ON SPIRITED yet WELL-BEHAVED ANIMALS... ANNIE LEIBOVITZ CALLED AS WELL... MICK AND the STONES WANT to DO AN ALBUM COVER WITH "S", "LJ", AND "Y." I SAID I WAS SURE they'd be DELIGHTED, but SECRETLY I THINK they WOULD PREFER A MICHAEL BOLTON ALBUM.

the Dogs from HELL Love to PARTY.

DIDN'T GET ENOUGH PARTY-ING LAST NIGHT?

Looking FOR the ULTIMATE PARTY THRILL?

Free Every-thing inside

ANYONE COMING?

SIX PAIRS OF BLOODSHOT EYES, WEARING PARTY HATS.

the DOGS FROM {e} try to Lure the prurient to the J. EDGAR HOOVER MEMORIAL LIBRARY AND CAFÉ.

We Got the DIRT ON EVERYONE AND it's in ALPHAbeTicAL ORDER! FREE COFFEE AND CROISSANTS! COME ON IN.

ANYONE COMING?

SOME REPORTERS AND A FEW CONGRESSMEN... LIGHT the BARBEQUE.

Worried about Muggers, but opposed to guns? order one of the SYLVIA Protector T-Shirts At riGHt. AvAilable in French cut only.

Doberman in Purse →

FISH IN SOCK

THE Dogs from HELL Are Looking FOR the SHORT-TERM COMPANIONSHIP of Smokers.

SMOKERS WELCOME!! Come on in... we'll treat you nice. we love the smell of smoke.

Anyone coming?

I HEAR COUGHING IN THE Distance.

Pet Care Instructions During the Renaissance.

Dear Lucrezia, THANKS SO MUCH FOR OFFERING to CARE FOR BRUNO WHILE I'M AWAY... you Are A dear, No MATTER WHAT ANY ONE SAYS. PLEASE MAKE SURE He HAS HIS "WALKIES" three times A DAY AND THAT He HAS PLENTY OF WATER. ALSO, PLEASE... DON'T POISON HIS FOOD. REMEMBER, He's A DOG, NOT A RELATIVE.

the **Dogs** from **HELL** try to entice some corporate playmates to their apartment.

FREE FAX, Scones, Cappuccino.

Step INSIDE

WELCOME!

ANYONE COMING?

GUY WITH A BRIEFCASE, WOMAN WEARING NYLONS, WHITE SOCKS AND REEBOKS APPROACHING RAPIDLY FROM THE LEFT.

the Woman who does Everything More Beautifully than you never wastes a morning sitting around the veterinarian's office.

Wednesday: took Suzie, LORD JEFF AND YEATS into the Vet's. AS SOON AS SHE HEARD I WAS THERE, DR. GREAT-HART RUSHED out to embrace me. SHE INSISTED THAT THERE BE NO CHARGE FOR the visit BECAUSE MY Pets Are SO ADORABLE AND WELL-BEHAVED, it's AN HONOR to treat them.

Home Home on the range... where the deer and the antelope play.

ABOUT THE AUTHOR

Nicole Hollander is the author of the syndicated cartoon strip *Sylvia*, which appears in more than eighty papers nationwide, including the *Chicago Tribune*, the *Boston Globe*, and the *L.A. Times.* Nicole lives in Chicago and shares her flat with two lovely guys, Buddy and Izzy.